VOLCANOLOGISTS

Robin Koontz

Rourke
Educational Media

rourkeeducationalmedia.com

*Scan for Related Titles
and Teacher Resources*

Before Reading:

Building Academic Vocabulary and Background Knowledge

Before reading a book, it is important to tap into what your child or students already know about the topic. This will help them develop their vocabulary, increase their reading comprehension, and make connections across the curriculum.

1. *Look at the cover of the book. What will this book be about?*
2. *What do you already know about the topic?*
3. *Let's study the Table of Contents. What will you learn about in the book's chapters?*
4. *What would you like to learn about this topic? Do you think you might learn about it from this book? Why or why not?*
5. *Use a reading journal to write about your knowledge of this topic. Record what you already know about the topic and what you hope to learn about the topic.*
6. *Read the book.*
7. *In your reading journal, record what you learned about the topic and your response to the book.*
8. *After reading the book complete the activities below.*

Content Area Vocabulary
Read the list. What do these words mean?

contiguous
ecosystem
gravity
hydrothermal
infrared
lava
magma
seismic
spectrometer
submersible
tsunami

After Reading:

Comprehension and Extension Activity

After reading the book, work on the following questions with your child or students in order to check their level of reading comprehension and content mastery.

1. *What fields should you study to become a volcanologist?* (Text to self connection)
2. *Why did the eruption of Mt. St. Helens trigger a greater need for volcano research?* (Asking questions)
3. *Why is it important to study past volcanic eruptions?* (Summarize)
4. *Explain how technology is changing volcanic research.* (Asking questions)
5. *What words did the author use to help you visualize a volcanic eruption?* (Visualize)

Extension Activity

Volcanoes were a mystery for thousands of years. Cultures all around the world have legends that explain volcanic eruptions. Research volcanic legends and read how various groups explain volcanic activity. Then write your own legend to explain how volcanoes are formed or why they erupt. Share your legend with your teacher, classmates, or family.

TABLE OF CONTENTS

KILLER MOUNTAIN

"Vancouver! Vancouver! This is it!" Those were the last words anyone heard from David Johnston. He was closely monitoring a steaming, trembling snow-capped mountain near Vancouver, Washington. Mount St. Helens had not erupted in more than 100 years. But two months earlier, an earthquake jolted it to life. Homes were evacuated and roads were closed as hundreds of explosive blasts of steam burst from the volcano. Earthquakes shook the area. Scientists knew pressure was building up inside the mountain. They could see the north side had grown outward almost 450 feet (140 meters). This was evidence that molten rock, called **magma**, had risen high into the volcano. They felt that a massive eruption could happen soon. But when?

1.

2.

On May 17, 1980, after two months of thousands of daily earthquakes and more steam blasts, the volcano was silent again. Many observers were there to watch the expected drama. They went home, thinking that the excitement was over.

But it wasn't.

On May 18, 1980, just seconds after David radioed those final words to his colleagues, the huge mountain blew itself apart in the worst volcanic event in the **contiguous** United States since 1915. His monitoring station was more than five miles (8 kilometers) away, which he considered a safe distance.

1. March 1980, small phreatic, or steam, explosions began.
2. April 1980, a "bulge" developed on the north side of Mount St. Helens as magma pushed up within the peak explosion.
3. May 1980, Mount St. Helens erupts in a massive explosion.

An aerial view of Mount St. Helens showing the Plinian eruption column.

A huge landslide bulldozed down the mountain at almost 700 miles (1,126 kilometers) per hour, crashing over everything in its path. Debris roared through the land below, as far as 14 miles (23 kilometers) west of the blast. The explosion that followed sent ash, magma, rocks and sand high into the air. David and his trailer were never found. It was assumed that both were engulfed by the blast and buried in the debris from the landslide. Fifty-six other people also were killed that day.

Immediately before the blast, an earthquake loosened the snow and soil on the north side of the volcano. Johnston was probably alerting his colleagues to the huge swell of dirt and snow that broke free and started rushing down the mountain.

The 1980 eruption of Mount St. Helens destroyed more than 230 square miles (370 square kilometers) of forests and the wildlife that lived there.

The ground covering had kept the volcano from releasing the building pressure. Now the mountain was free to explode, and that's what it did.

For the next nine hours, ash and magma spewed thousands of feet up in a three mile (4.8 kilometer) wide plume. People 30 miles (48 kilometers) away reported that burned pinecones and pebbles rained down around them. The day started with the largest landslide in recorded history and ended with a devastating volcanic eruption that spread ash and debris over thousands of miles of landscape. It took many years for the area to recover.

Even though the eruption of Mount St. Helens was a disastrous event, it did some good. It taught scientists an important link between earthquakes and volcanic activity. Some refer to the eruption of Mount St. Helens as the "dawn of earthquake science in the United States."

Left: This photo of Mount St. Helens was taken a day before the May 1980 eruption. Middle and Right: The volcano after the eruption with a line showing what disappeared.

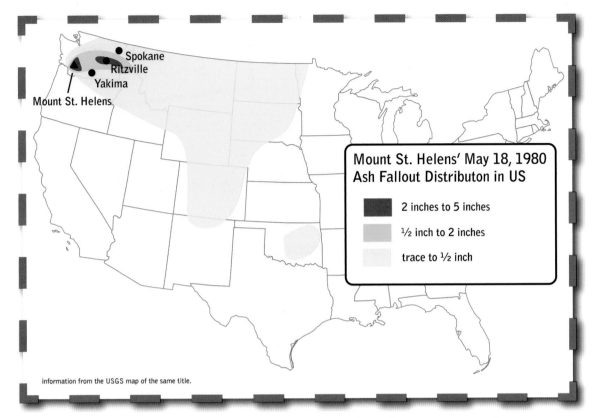

Map showing the distribution of ash fallout after the 1980 eruption.

Since that terrible day, scientists have learned a lot about how volcanoes grow and change, as well as how they are linked to earthquakes. Scientists like David, who lost his life monitoring Mount St. Helens, are a brave bunch. They are called volcanologists. Volcanologists may have the most dangerous job in the field of science.

Mount St. Helens is recharging and will erupt again, according to John Ewert, a volcanologist at the USGS Cascades Volcano Observatory in Vancouver, Washington. It is one of the most active volcanoes in the world.

A volcanologist installs a GPS receiver on a benchmark near the crater of Mount St. Helens.

WHAT IS A VOLCANOLOGIST?

Volcanoes have been feared, admired, and even worshipped by some cultures. Many times their eruptions have been unexpected and often deadly. Volcanic activity has destroyed entire cities and killed thousands of people.

Tungurahua, an active volcano in Ecuador

A volcano can appear in different shapes and sizes. Generally it is a hill or mountain that has a crater or vents where molten material once erupted. It is usually cone-shaped, but not always.

Volcanic activity can reshape the land. It can form mountains and create new landscapes. The ash and debris that volcanoes spread nurtures the soil, creating fertile ground for plants and wildlife. People will often live in the shadow of a volcano because of the rich soil for growing food crops. People also harness the heat energy that comes from some volcanic systems.

For thousands of years, volcanoes were a mysterious, sensational, and often dangerous part of the world's landscape. But then people began to study volcanoes, trying to figure out what makes them tick. They wanted to discover how volcanoes formed and especially what causes them to erupt.

The study of volcanoes became a special interest for many geologists. They were called volcanologists. Volcanology specifically studies the processes that affect the magma flow and eruption through vents on the surface of the Earth.

Volcanologists usually get a college degree in geology, geochemistry, or geophysics. Then they specialize in volcanoes. In general, geology deals with the Earth's physical structure. Geochemistry focuses on the chemical composition of the Earth. Geophysics deals with understanding Earth's geology by using physics and mathematics.

Scientists swarmed over the area after the eruption of Mount St. Helens, gathering data and studying debris deposits.

Volcanologists specialize in different areas that are related to volcanoes. Physical volcanologists gather data and study actual volcanic eruptions and their deposits. They map the deposits that make up the volcano and collect samples to analyze. By dating and identifying the volcanic samples, they learn about the volcano's history.

Geophysics is another branch of volcanology. These scientists study the frequency of earthquakes close to a volcano. They also study and analyze a volcano's **gravity** and magnetics.

Geodesic volcanologists study how the shape of the Earth changes from volcanic eruptions. Geochemists can also become volcanologists. They study what a volcano produces, including magma and gases.

Volcanologists rarely perch on the lip of an erupting volcano to do their research. Most of their work is done studying dead or dormant volcanoes. They monitor active volcanoes around the world from observatories. But they will also monitor volcanoes that appear to be awakening.

Scientists collect gas samples around Mount St. Helens to check for changes in the chemical composition.

Volcanologists sometimes spend several months a year living in a tent. They collect samples, make notes, check instruments, and take photographs. Recording data is an important part of the job, as it is with any scientific research.

USGS scientist Cynthia Gardner gathers rock samples from the new growth on the dome of Mount St. Helens.

Volcanologists share their findings with other scientists. They have a common goal. They hope to predict where, how, and when a volcano is likely to erupt.

Richard Fiske is a world-famous volcanologist. He once said, "Once you get started in volcanoes, you become a junkie. The Earth is changing and you try to outfox it, understand its past activity and predict what it's likely to do in the future."

TOOLS OF THE TRADE

Volcanologists use all kinds of equipment for their research and monitoring. Here are a few of their tools:

A thermal **infrared** camera can monitor the temperature of emissions from a volcano.

A tiltmeter can measure a volcano's slope and detect even the smallest change.

A radar mapping instrument creates detailed maps of the Earth's surface. It helps scientists predict where **lava** flow and other products from a volcano might travel.

A **spectrometer** can analyze light that comes through a volcanic plume from a safe distance. The light helps to identify the kind of gases coming out of the volcano.

A **seismic** monitor can be used to measure earthquake activity close to a volcano.

Earthquakes are measured at seismic monitoring stations throughout the world.

LEARNING FROM THE PAST

Mount Vesuvius looms behind the ruins of Pompeii, Italy.

A volcano in Italy called Vesuvius exploded in 79 CE. The debris from the devastating blast completely buried the city of Pompeii along with other Roman towns and farms around the Bay of Naples.

Archaeologists and volcanologists have studied the area for many years. The best account of the eruption they have are two letters written by a young man named Pliny the Younger. The young historian described the event in great detail.

Pliny lived in a city close enough to see and experience the volcano's eruption. He told about the earthquakes that preceded the blast. He reported all that he observed as the cloud of ash and gases exploded and spread. He described the plumes emitted from the volcano. He wrote of lava flows and the **tsunami** triggered by the earthquakes and eruption.

He also told how he and his mother were nearly buried in ash and his uncle, Pliny the Elder, was killed. Pliny's detailed observations provided valuable information to volcanologists about the historic event. It was the first detailed, scientific description of a volcanic eruption ever recorded. Pliny the Younger is considered by many to be the first volcanologist.

FIELD NOTES

Volcanologists describe large volcanic eruption clouds of rock, ash, and gases as Plinian in honor of the young historian. The 1980 eruption of Mount St. Helens is an example of a Plinian eruption.

In the 1700s, the ancient city of Pompeii was slowly uncovered and evidence of the terrible event revealed. Archaeologists found the charred remains of people buried in layers of volcanic ash and pumice.

The position of the bodies caused the scientists to believe they had suffocated or were slowly burned alive. But thanks to a volcanologist named Giuseppe Mastrolorenzo and his research team, this turned out to be incorrect.

The team analyzed the many layers of ash and rock from the eruption. The data was fed into a computer. The computer used the data to simulate the eruption of Mount Vesuvius. The results gave the scientists valuable information about what happened.

They learned from their data and the computer simulations that the people of Pompeii had been exposed to extremely high temperatures. They were burned instantly by a surge of heat. It was possibly more than 570 degrees Fahrenheit (300 degrees Celsius). The scientists compared the results with other studies that tested metal silverware that melted.

"Heretofore archaeologists misinterpreted them as people struggling to breathe and believed they died suffocated by ashes," Mastrolorenzo said. "Now we know that couldn't be."

FIELD NOTES

Mount Vesuvius is still an active volcano. More violent eruptions occurred in the late 1700s, 1800s, and early 1900s. The most recent eruption was in 1944. The area has more than a million people living in the danger zone. San Sebastiano sits directly on top of the lava that destroyed the city in the 1944 eruption.

Mount Vesuvius is one of the most closely watched volcanoes in the world. Claudio Scarpati is a volcanologist involved with the Vesuvius observatory in Naples. Data from sensors pointed at the volcano are constantly analyzed. He and other scientists hope that they can warn people far ahead of time if Mount Vesuvius is about to erupt again.

Mount Vesuvius is the only volcano on the European mainland that has erupted during the past century and is still active. It has erupted more than 50 times during the past 2,000 years.

FIELD NOTES

The World Organization of Volcano Observatories (WOVO) has about 70 member organizations. Members are observatories in charge of keeping the public notified about possible volcanic activity. WOVO helps with communication and cooperation between all the observatories. It also refers those seeking assistance to the appropriate member observatory.

IN THE MOUTH OF
THE MONSTER

Volcanologists want to understand the nature of volcanoes They are among the most adventurous researchers in the field science. Volcanologists often find themselves getting extremel close to a volcano, despite the potential dangers.

VOLCANOES ARE PUT INTO THREE CLASSES:

- **active**, which means it has erupted at least once during the past 10,000 years.
- **dormant**, which is still an active volcano but hasn't erupted in several hundred years. It could show signs such as escaping gas.
- **extinct**, which is a volcano that hasn't erupted or shown any signs of activity for at least 10,000 years and is unlikely to ever erupt again.

There are various methods used in fieldwork. In addition to mapping areas and collecting rocks, volcanologists drill for core samples. All of the materials are analyzed later. They identify t materials and determine their age by using radiocarbon dating

A Real-Time Kinematic (RTK) Global Positioning System (GPS) surveying system can accurately monitor changes inside the Mount St. Helens crater.

The scientists also document changes in the volcano. They watch for new fractures or gas vents and other new features. Seismic activity is measured with instruments installed over the volcano. They also measure the crater to see if it has grown bigger. Tiltmeters are placed on the ground to measure changes.

A tiltmeter measures the slope angle of the ground. It is an old method to monitor the smallest changes caused by moving magma. The modern electronic tiltmeter can continuously record ground tilts.

Scientists might also set up webcams and other imaging devices to record activity. These instruments can be monitored from a safe distance. Some surveys can be done from a helicopter or by a Global Positioning System (GPS) from an aircraft or satellite.

Dr. Clive Oppenheimer is professor of volcanology at Cambridge University in Great Britain. One of his projects is studying a volcano on Ross Island, Antarctica. He spends one month every year monitoring Mount Erebus, an active volcano.

Mount Erebus

The -22 Fahrenheit (-30 Celsius) temperatures don't bother the volcanologist as he analyzes the gases that come out of the volcano. He points a spectrometer into the gaping opening of Mount Erebus so that he can analyze its lava lake. He hopes his research will help explain why some volcanoes explode violently, while others erupt more peacefully.

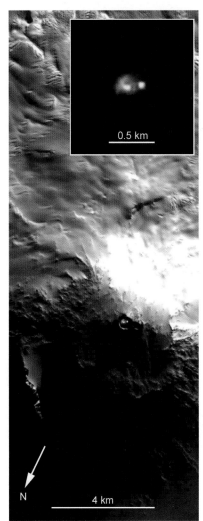

0.5 km

N   4 km

Satellite view of the lava lake on Mount Erebus.

"There are plenty of other volcanoes all around the world that I could go to, but Erebus is very special ... I think it's the closest I could imagine to being an astronaut and going to Mars or somewhere very exotic," Dr. Oppenheimer said.

In Hawaii, volcanologists and other researchers study Kilauea, a fairly calm but active volcano that has erupted almost constantly since 1960. It is the most active volcano in the world. The eruptions are fairly low-key, so the scientists are somewhat safe as they study the activity. They observe and document the lava and behavior of the eruptions. Lava samples are taken to study the chemistry and temperature. They also work with the Hawaii County Civil Defense to warn the public of any dangers.

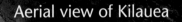
Aerial view of Kilauea

The ways volcanologists peer inside a volcano are often dangerous. But their extensive research and data collecting helps the scientific community better understand volcanoes.

A USGS scientist carefully measures the lava temperature on Kilauea.

"When you're looking at a volcano, it's like you're looking at a tailpipe of a car when you really want to see the engine. Most of the processes are hidden from view in Earth's crust," said George Bergantz, geologist at the University of Washington.

The Yellowstone volcano, located in Yellowstone National Park, is a popular tourist attraction. It is actually a caldera, a sunken pit that was formed by the collapse or explosion of the center of a volcano. Not all visitors understand that Yellowstone is an active volcano. There are 1,000 to 3,000 earthquakes per year, constant changes in the ground and more than 10,000 thermal features. Volcanologists and other scientists have monitored the caldera closely for more than 30 years. Monitors placed throughout the region keep them informed of any increasing activity or changes.

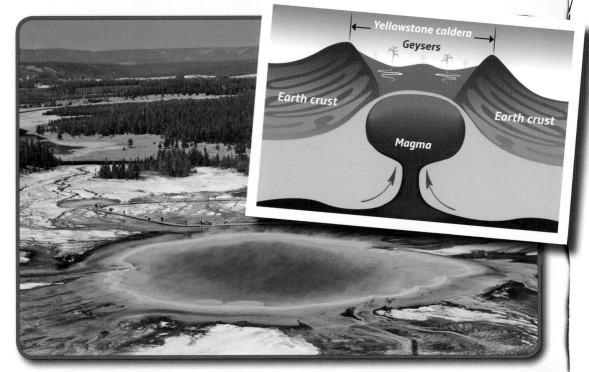

Grand Prismatic Spring in Yellowstone National Park

SUBMARINE VOLCANO SCIENTISTS

More than half of the Earth's volcanic activity is hidden deep in the ocean. Exploring these submarine volcanoes requires a team effort. Marine biologists, volcanologists, and chemists join forces to learn about these rumbling beasts of the deep.

The Ring of Fire is a string of volcanoes and earthquake sites around the edges of the Pacific Ocean, both above and below the ocean's surface. The Ring of Fire is the result of plate tectonics. Tectonic plates are slabs of the Earth's crust that fit together somewhat like puzzle pieces. Sometimes the plates collide, slide together, or move apart. This tectonic activity can create earthquakes and volcanic activity.

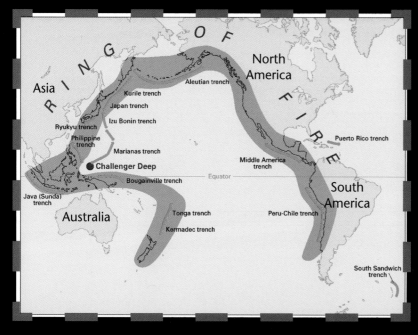

Mount St. Helens is a volcano in the Ring of Fire.

It is more difficult to study underwater volcanoes. But in recent years, scientists have been helped by some amazing undersea equipment.

The National Oceanic and Atmospheric Administration (NOAA) set up an underwater observatory in the Ring of Fire near an active volcano called Axial Seamount. The observatory, New Millennium Observatory (NeMO), collects data from instruments guided by teams of scientists.

Seamounts are undersea mountains formed by volcanic activity. This is a map of a seamount in the Arctic Ocean created by gathering data with a multibeam echo sounder.

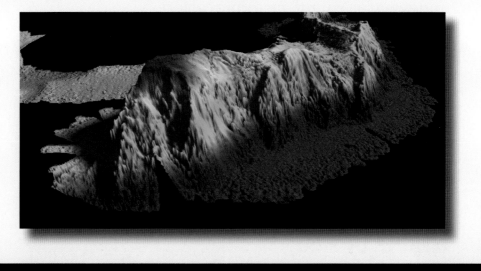

The ongoing project uses remote **submersibles** and other instruments to collect data. Robert Embley, a geophysicist, and other scientists involved with NeMO hope to continue studying the area for many years. Each expedition brings new information about activities of deep-sea volcanoes.

One very useful underwater helper is a Remotely Operated Platform for Ocean Science (ROPOS). It has equipment such as video cameras, sensors, suction samplers, sonar, and robotic arms that gather samples from inside and around a volcano. ROPOS is transported inside a steel cage that is lowered down to the exploration site. Then ROPOS leaves the cage and does its work. The machine is expensive to transport but is used for all kinds of underwater scientific exploration.

ROPOS manipulator arm

Robert Ballard is an oceanographer and deep-sea explorer. He is known for discovering the wreck of the Titanic and other shipwrecks around the world. Robert was also part of the 1979 exploration team that documented **hydrothermal** vents in the ocean floor soon after they were discovered.

Hydrothermal vents are seafloor hot springs. They occur in places where submarine volcanoes erupt lava or bring hot magma close to the surface.

He and a team of scientists have studied Kick'em Jenny, an active and potentially dangerous submarine volcano in the Caribbean Sea. Kick'em Jenny was discovered in 1939, and has erupted about 12 times since then.

Kick'em Jenny is so dangerous that the scientists used a Remotely Operated Vehicle (ROV) named Hercules to explore the volcano. Hercules was a submersible that could record what was going on in and around the volcano. The scientists were amazed to see that sea creatures lived inside the volcano.

They guided Hercules to create maps, collect samples, including living organisms, and take photos.

The information from these undersea expeditions provides volcanologists clues about how submarine volcanoes develop and their relationship with the ocean's **ecosystem**.

Hercules, a remotely operated vehicle, can descend to depths of 2.5 miles (4,000 meters).

In August of 1883, the island volcano Krakatau erupted in one of the most deadly natural disasters in modern history. At least 36,400 people were killed. Most were killed by a tsunami triggered by the exploding mountain as it collapsed into the sea. Krakatau is now a caldera submarine volcano, and is still active.

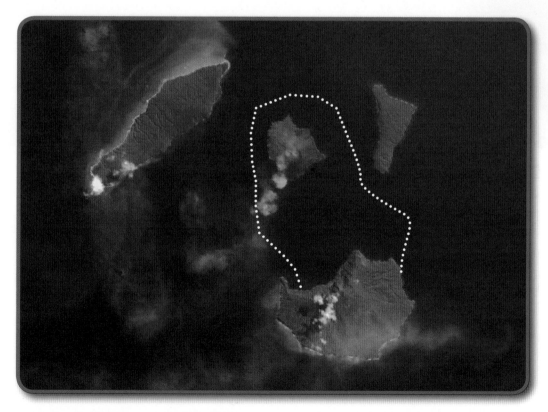

The 1883 eruption of Krakatau wiped out two-thirds of the original island.

PREDICTING DISASTER

A geochemist measures natural volcanic air pollution (vog) using an instrument that can detect gas compositions based on the absorbed infrared light.

Much of the work done by volcanologists is fueled by the need to predict a catastrophic volcanic event such as the 1980 eruption of Mount St. Helens. Understanding more about volcanoes makes it easier to forecast an eruption.

Ground sensors detect changes in the shape of the volcano. Gas monitors and other instruments detect changes in volcanic gas emissions. Satellite radar can record when the landscape around the volcano changes.

Volcanologists constantly compare data and readings to help determine when a volcano is going to erupt. They know that magma and gas are getting closer to the surface if instruments detect more earthquakes. Emissions of sulfur dioxide, CO_2, and other gases are also clues that volcanic action is looming. The data collected and shared by volcanologists worldwide have advanced the knowledge of how all volcanoes behave.

Geochemist Jeff Sutton shows volcanology students from around the world instruments that measure volcanic gases on Mount Kilauea.

FIELD NOTES

There are always new ideas for even better instruments to analyze volcanoes, such as infrared telescopes and infrared spectrometers to identify volcanic gases. Dr. Stanley Williams, a volcanologist who was nearly killed by a volcano in 1993, is designing an instrument that has tiny electrochemical sensors that can detect and automatically transmit data about volcanic gases in the air.

Florian (Max) Schwandner is a geochemist whose work includes monitoring gas emissions from active volcanoes. When asked about the monitoring efforts of The World Organization of Volcano Observatories (WOVO), he responded that, "The success rate over the last several decades has been tremendous. We have 70 percent accuracy on the two-week time margin by some accounts, which is better than storm forecasting."

Before the 1980 eruption of Mount St. Helens, there was only one volcano observatory in the US, in Hawaii. Scientists there watch over 100 active volcanoes. Now there are observatories in many other places around the world. The United States Geological Survey (USGS) has about 100 volcanologists on staff.

A scientist at the Alaska Volcano Observatory notes earthquakes developing near an erupting volcano.

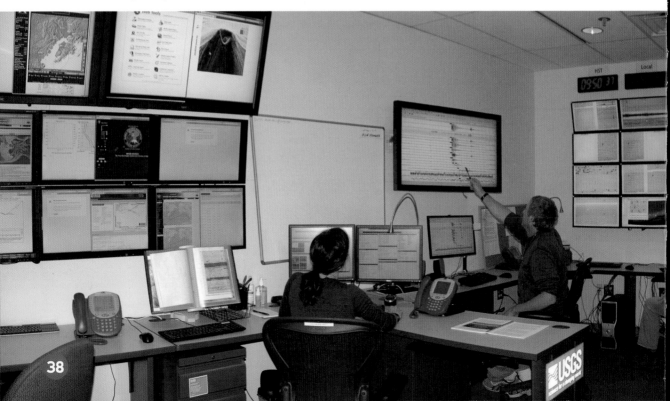

There is no doubt that volcanologists have saved thousands of lives. Sometimes they risk their lives while saving others. David Johnston, the volcanologist who perished at Mount St. Helens, is credited with saving up to 20,000 lives. He was one of the scientists who insisted that the evacuation remain in place, even though the mountain appeared to have become quiet.

This is a high-resolution satellite image of Calbuco, a volcano in southern Chile, as it erupted on April 23, 2015. The photo was captured by a scanning radiometer called Visible Infrared Imaging Radiometer Suite (VIIRS).

FIELD NOTES

"There are 169 volcanoes in the US that have erupted in the last 10,000 years," said Jeff Wynn, chief scientist of the USGS volcano hazards program. "That means they could become active again with very little warning."

A skylight, such as the West Kamokuna Skylight, is an opening in the roof above a lava tube.

In 1991, Mount Pinatubo in the Philippines began to stir. It was dormant for about 500 years, and thousands of people lived nearby. When the once quiet mountain showed evidence of an impending eruption, volcanologists from the Philippines and the US joined forces.

The scientists analyzed evidence from previous eruptions. The ancient deposits helped them determine the type of eruption to expect. They installed instruments to measure ground changes, gases, and seismic activity.

The eruption in 1991 of Mount Pinatubo was the second largest eruption of the 20th century. It was 10 times larger than the 1980 Mount St. Helens eruption.

The scientists determined that a volcanic eruption from Mount Pinatubo had the potential to threaten thousands of people, and it was about to blow. There was no time to lose. About 75,000 people were evacuated.

Shortly after the evacuation, the eruptions began, lasting for several days. There was extensive damage from the ash and mudflows, but the evacuation saved many lives.

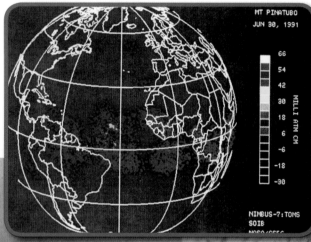

A Total Ozone Mapping Spectrometer (TOMS) image shows ash circling the Earth from Mount Pinatubo's 1991 eruption.

An aerial view of the caldera of Mount Pinatubo on June 22, 1991.

The American scientists were a Volcano Disaster Assistance Program (VDAP) team. Upon invitation, VDAP sends teams and portable monitoring equipment to respond to eruptions and volcanic unrest. VDAP is backed by the larger USGS Volcano Hazards Program (VHP). VHP provides extra staff and support when it is needed.

But meanwhile, the team is always standing by, ready to help monitor potential volcanic activity anywhere in the world. Considering there are more than 1,500 potentially active volcanoes on the planet, it's good to know that help is ready.

FIELD NOTES

When not responding to a crisis, VDAP works with international partners to build volcano-monitoring networks. They also assist with education programs in eruption forecasting and assessment.

VDAP's home is based in the Cascades Volcano Observatory in Vancouver, Washington. It's no surprise that such a valuable team has its home near the volcano that started it all: Mount St. Helens.

TIMELINE

August 24, 79 CE
Mount Vesuvius exploded, destroying entire cities and farm communities. The detailed account by Pliny the Younger marked the beginning of volcanology.

1841
The first volcano observatory opened on the flanks of Mount Vesuvius.

Frank A. Perret (1867 - 1943)
helped to better define volcanology in the 20th century through his detailed research of several active volcanoes around the world.

1922
The first journal of volcano research, *Bulletin Volcanologique*, was published.

Haroun Tazieff (1914-1998)
was the first volcanologist to capture the beauty of volcanoes in spectacular documentary films, making volcanoes familiar to millions of television viewers for the first time.

May 18, 1980
The eruption of Mount St. Helens pushed volcanology into a more important level of science.

WAYS TO GET IN THE FIELD

There are only about a thousand volcanologists in the world today, though the number is growing. It can be a dangerous job, but it's a very valuable part of scientific research. If you want to get involved, study geology and other science subjects, including chemistry.

Read books about geology and volcanoes. Take math and physics classes. If you can, travel to a real volcano and visit the observatory.

Writing is a big part of a volcanologist's job. You want to be able to explain complex things to the public so they understand the dangers of a potential volcanic eruption. Learning how to write grants for funding is also a much-needed skill in volcanology and other research fields.

Volcanologists work in observatories and in the field. They might teach others in colleges and universities. But all volcanologists share a passion for studying one of the most fascinating and hazardous wonders of nature: volcanoes.

Glossary

contiguous (kun-TIG-yoo-us): sharing an edge or a boundary

ecosystem (EK-oh-siss-tuhm): a community of animals and plants interacting with their environment

gravity (grav-uh-tee): the force that pulls things down toward the surface of the Earth

hydrothermal (hye-druh-THUR-mul): of or relating to hot water

infrared (in-fruh-RED): producing or using rays of light that cannot be seen and that are longer than rays that produce red light

lava (LAH-vuh): magma that was released from a volcano

magma (MAG-muh): hot, liquid rock found beneath the Earth's surface

seismic (SIZE-mik): of, relating to, or caused by an earthquake

spectrometer (spek-TROM-uh-tur): an instrument used for measuring wavelengths of light

submersibles (sub-MUR-suh-buhls): small vehicles that can operate underwater and that are used especially for research

tsunami (tsoo-NAH-mee): a very large wave usually caused by an underwater volcano or earthquake

Index

Show What You Know

1. Why is volcanology a branch of geology?
2. What are some of the instruments used by volcanologists?
3. What tests do volcanologists conduct to predict if a volcano might erupt?
4. Why is an organism that lives inside a submarine volcano so unusual? What can we learn from them?
5. What kinds of scientists besides volcanologists get involved in studying volcanoes?

Websites to Visit

www.see.leeds.ac.uk/afar/new-afar/day-in-life/day-volc.html

www.pmel.noaa.gov/eoi/nemo/explorer.html

www.volcanolive.com/index.html

About the Author

Robin Koontz is a freelance author/illustrator/ designer of a wide variety of nonfiction and fiction books, educational blogs, and magazine articles for children and young adults. Her 2011 science title, *Leaps and Creeps - How Animals Move to Survive,* was an Animal Behavior Society Outstanding Children's Book Award Finalist. Raised in Maryland and Alabama, Robin now lives with her husband in the Coast Range of western Oregon where she especially enjoys observing the wildlife on her property. You can learn more on her blog, robinkoontz.wordpress.com.

Meet The Author!
www.meetREMauthors.com

www.rourkeeducationalmedia.com

PHOTO CREDITS: Cover and page 1: volcano © Fotos593, volcanologist © Nikitin Victor, smoke © Trifonenko Ivan. Orsk; page 4 both photos courtesy of USGS, page 5 courtesy of NOAA News Photo; pages 6-8 courtesy of USGS; page 9 top © Murraybuckley, page 10 and throughout, burnt paper © spaxiax, page 10 photo courtesy USGS, page 11 © Fotos593; page 12-13 © Ammit Jack; page 14-17 courtesy USGS; page 18-19 © Sailorr; page 20-21 © balounm; page 25 courtesy of USGS; page 26 © es0teric, page 27 courtesy of NASA; page 28 © Amy Nichole Harris, page 29 illustration © Linar, photo © Lorcel; page 30 map courtesy of USGS, page 31-34 courtesy of NOAA; page 32 Image courtesy of Submarine Ring of Fire 2002, NOAA/OER; page 35 satellite photo courtesy of NASA; page 36 and 37 courtesy of USGS; page 38 and 40 courtesy of USGS, , page 39 courtesy of NOAA; page 41-45 courtesy of USGS, inset photo page 42 courtesy of NASA

Edited by: Keli Sipperley

Cover and Interior design by: Nicola Stratford   www.nicolastratford.com

Library of Congress PCN Data

Volcanologists / Robin Koontz
(Scientists in the Field)
ISBN 978-1-63430-409-2 (hard cover)
ISBN 978-1-63430-509-9 (soft cover)
ISBN 978-1-63430-601-0 (e-Book)
Library of Congress Control Number: 2015931709

Printed in the United States of America, North Mankato, Minnesota

Also Available as:

ROURKE'S
e-Books